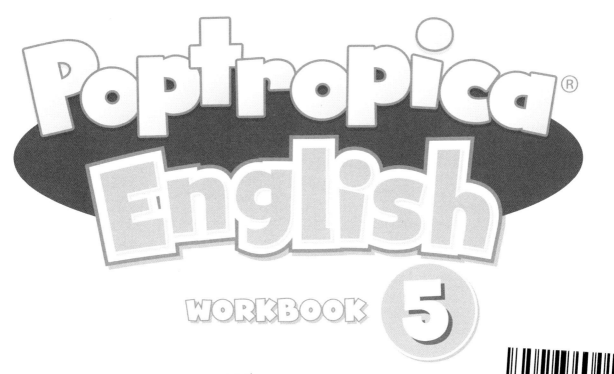

WORKBOOK 5

José Luis Morales • Laura Miller • John Wiltshier
Series advisor: David Nunan

Pearson Education Limited
Edinburgh Gate
Harlow
Essex CM20 2JE
England
and Associated Companies throughout the world.

Poptropica English

© Pearson Education Limited 2015

Based on the work of Laura Miller

The rights of Laura Miller, John Wiltshier, and José Luis Morales to be identified as authors of this work have been asserted by them in accordance with the Copyright, Designs and Patents Act 1988.

Design, editorial and project management by hyphen

First published 2015
Fourteenth impression 2024

ISBN: 978-1-292-09133-4

Set in Fiendstar 13/20pt

Printed in Slovakia by Neografia

Illustrators: Charlotte Alder (The Bright Agency), Illias Arahovitis (Beehive Illustration), Fred Blunt, Lawrence Christmas, Leo Cultura, Mark Draisey, John Martz, Rob, McClurkan (Beehive), Ken Mok, Zaharias Papadopoulos (hyphen), Jim Peacock (Beehive Illustration), Christos Skaltsas (hyphen) and Olimpia Wong.

The publisher would like to thank the following for their kind permission to reproduce their photographs:

(Key: b-bottom; c-centre; l-left; r-right; t-top)

123RF.com: Destinacigdem 20 (skateboard), Glenda Powers 79cl, Yury Salauyou 35, sergein 23b, vladzoco 43tl, Cathy Yeulet 43tc, zigt 33tr; **Alamy Images:** Design Pictures Inc. 53tc, FineArt 15, Philip Lee Harvey 79tr, ImageBROKER 53tl, 83tl, Imagemore Co., Ltd 79cr, Juice Images 83cr, Lohkee 83tr, MBI 53tr, Oxana Oleynichenko 81t, Myrleen Pearson 79bl, PhotosIndia.com LLC 79br, Spotmatik 33cl, Westend61 GmbH 20bl; **Brand X Pictures:** photolibrary.com 34; **Creatas:** 43tr/2; **Digital Vision:** 45tr; **Fotolia.com:** Boggy 76, CandyBox Images 23cr, Driving South 79tl; **Getty Images:** AFP / Yasuyoshi Chiba 81c, Caiaimage / Tom Merton 75, NBAE / Rocky Widner 81b; **MedioImages:** 21b; **Pearson Education Ltd:** Jon Barlow 20 (Jamie), 20 (Sasha), 20tr, 21t; **Shutterstock.com:** 20b, Ashwin 23cl, AVAVA 43tr/1, Blend Images 6cl, 43bl, Ana Bokan 6c/2, Colman Lerner Gerardo 39, cowardlion 33b, Creatista 43br, Joca de Jong 43cl, Erashov 33t, Alexander Fediachov 20 (ball), Happy Together 33cr, Incredible Arctic 45tc, iofoto 83cl, JHDT Stock Images LLC. 6cr/2, Kameel4u 23c, Leungchopan 6cr, MadamLEAD 43cr, Monkey Business Images 6cl/2, 23t, Odua Images 6c/1

All other images © Pearson Education Limited

Every effort has been made to trace the copyright holders and we apologize in advance for any unintentional omissions. We would be pleased to insert the appropriate acknowledgement in any subsequent edition of this publication.

Contents

Welcome

1 **Write. Who are they?**

> Gizmo   Hector Frost   Mike   Polly   Polly's mom   Smith   The Queen of Ice Island

1

2

3

4

_____

5

6

7

_____

2 **Look at Activity 1 and number the sentences.**

a He's wearing boots and a hat. He likes soccer, adventures, and dogs. `4`

b He's tall and thin. He's rich and he likes diamonds and dogs. ☐

c He's bald. He likes driving a skidoo and he's strong. ☐

d She's beautiful and rich. She has a diamond necklace. ☐

e She likes adventure and solving problems. She has long, black hair. ☐

f He's black and white. He's wearing a green collar around his neck. ☐

g She has a daughter and she likes to cook. ☐

3 **Look and check (✓).**

1 What does Polly hear?

a   **b**   **c**

□   □   □

2 Who gets the diamonds?

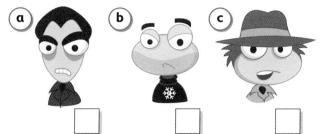

a   **b**   **c**

□   □   □

4 **Circle T = True or F = False.**

1 Polly and Mike wake up in the middle of the night.   T / F

2 A red ribbon falls off the skidoo outside Polly's home.   T / F

3 Polly's mom asks the children to read the newspapers.   T / F

4 Polly's name is Polly Jones.   T / F

5 The diamonds were in the town.   T / F

6 The thieves steal the diamonds in the day.   T / F

5 🎧 **Listen and match. Then write.**

1 What's Mike doing?   _____

2 What's Polly doing?   _____

3 What's Smith doing?   _____

6 Write.

1 She is _____ .

2 They _____ baseball.

3 _____

4 _____

5 _____

6 _____

7 _____

8 _____ the piano.

7 Listen and match.

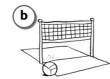  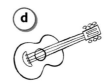 

8 Look at Activity 7 and write.

1 She _____ to music on Monday morning.

2 He _____ English on Thursday morning.

3 They _____ volleyball on Saturday afternoon.

4 She _____ a soccer game on Wednesday evening.

5 They _____ to the park on Sunday afternoon.

6 He _____ the guitar on Tuesday evening.

9 Write the days.

1   Yesterday was _____. Today is Tuesday.

2   Today is Saturday. Tomorrow is _____.

3   Two days ago was _____. Today is Thursday.

10 Write the years.

Now it's 20 __ __. Two years ago it was 20 __ __.

11   Listen and match. Then write.

1	2	3	4	5

(on Monday morning)   (two years ago)   (three days ago)

(two weeks ago)   (yesterday)

1   She _____ at school _____.

2   He _____.

3   They _____.

4   She _____ that _____.

5   They _____.

12 Write about yourself.

1   I _____ yesterday.

2   I _____ on _____.

3   I _____ ago.

⭐   Are you ready for Unit 1?

1 Friends

1 Unscramble and write.

Hair:

1 hgilt raih _____

2 ladb _____

3 yksip iarh _____

4 kdra hria _____

Face:

5 etcu _____

6 mdnaheos _____

7 odgo-gkolnio _____

8 auultibef _____

2 Write. Use words from Activity 1.

1
I have _____ hair.

Emma

2
I have _____ hair.

Maddy

3
I have _____ hair.

Robbie

4
I am _____.

Dan

3 Write one more sentence for each picture in Activity 2.

1 _____

2 _____

3 _____

4 _____

4 Unscramble and write questions.

1 does / look / what / she / like _____

2 look / what / do / like / they _____

3 look / does / he / what / like _____

5 Circle. Then check (✓) the true sentences.

1 He (is / has) bald. ☐

2 He (is / has) long, straight hair. ☐

1 She (has / is) beautiful. ☐

2 She (has / is) glasses. ☐

1 They (are / have) tall. ☐

2 They (are / have) short, curly hair. ☐

6 🎧 05 Listen and write.

	Dad	Mom	Grandpa
hair	**bald**		
eyes			
other			

7 Write sentences about the people in Activity 6.

1 Dad is bald. He has _____.

2 Mom _____ _____.

3 Grandpa _____.

8 Match.

1   She has a lot of friends because

2   She has a lot of friends but

3   She has a lot of friends and

4   I'm tall because

5   I'm tall but

6   I'm tall and

a   she doesn't have any brothers or sisters.

b   she has a lot of pets.

c   she's funny and creative.

d   I have straight, black hair.

e   my mom and dad are tall.

f   I'm not two meters tall!

9 Read and check (✓).

What makes a good friend?

	a good friend	don't mind	a bad friend
1 This person is friendly.	☐	☐	☐
2 This person isn't kind.	☐	☐	☐
3 This person is smart.	☐	☐	☐
4 This person isn't talkative.	☐	☐	☐
5 This person is bossy.	☐	☐	☐
6 This person is shy.	☐	☐	☐
7 This person isn't sporty.	☐	☐	☐
8 This person is lazy.	☐	☐	☐
9 This person is helpful.	☐	☐	☐
10 This person is hard-working.	☐	☐	☐

10 What makes a good or bad friend? Write using words from Activity 9.

A good friend _____.

A bad friend _____.

10   Lesson 3   Sing. (See Student Book page 14).

06

11 **Listen and match. Then write.**

1  Dan

2  Emma

3  Maddy

4  Robbie

smart / lazy

sporty / talkative

friendly / talkative

helpful / hard-working

1 What's Dan like? He's _____ and _____.

2 What's _____? She's _____ but she isn't _____ in class.

3 _____? She's _____ but a little _____.

4 _____? He's _____ and _____.

12 **Circle.**

1 I like my new teacher (because / but) she's patient.

2 He's hard-working (and / but) smart.

3 My best friend is creative (and / but) very friendly. She's great!

4 She doesn't get good grades (because / but) she's lazy.

5 He's lazy at home (but / and) he's hard-working in class.

6 She's smart (because / but) very bossy. I don't like her.

13 **Write about two friends at school.**

1 _____

2 _____

14 Write.

Hector Frost   Mike   Polly   Smith

①

②

③

④

_____ _____ _____ _____

15 Look at the story and check (✓).

1 Who are Mike and Polly following?

ⓐ ☐   ⓑ ☐   ⓒ ☐

2 Why? What did Polly hear at 2:00 a.m.?

ⓐ ☐   ⓑ ☐   ⓒ ☐

16 Find the words in the story and write.

1 These two words mean "Let's go."   _____

2 Hair growing on a man's face.   _____

3 People who steal.   _____

4 An idea for what to do next.   _____

5 A red fruit.   _____

6 To walk behind someone.   _____

17 Imagine. What happens next in the story?

I think _____ .

18 What do you say to help your friends? Number.

1 Do you want to review for the test?

2 10/10. Good job!

3 Can I help you?

4 I like your drawing.

1

a

b

c

d

19 Are you a good friend? Draw or stick a picture of yourself. Then write your own online profile.

20  **Listen and match.**

1   Megan   **2**   Seb's mom and dad   **3**   The food   **4**   Carlos

nice

happy

bossy

funny

creative

21 **Imagine you are staying with this family in the United States.
Write to a friend.**

○ ○ ○

From: _____

To: _____

Subject: | My stay in the United States

Dear _____,

I'm having a _____ time here in the
United States.

Emily is _____.
She has _____.

Steven is _____.
He has _____.

Their mom is _____.
She has _____.

Love,

_____

Emily   Steven

22 **Write.**

> Warm colors = yellow, _____ , _____ , _____ , _____

> Cool colors = green, _____ , _____ , _____ , _____

23 **Think and write.**

> ~~a banana~~ a giraffe a hippo a lake a lion
> a peach a tomato an elephant ~~grass~~ the ocean

warm colors
_____ a banana _____
_____
_____
_____
_____

cold colors
_____ grass _____
_____
_____
_____
_____

24 **Look and write.**

> curly mustache picture short thin young 28 1500

This [1]_____ is of artist Albrecht Durer
from Germany. Durer painted this picture in
[2]_____ . In this picture he has a long,
[3]_____ face. He has long, [4]_____
hair. He has a [5]_____ beard and a
[6]_____ , too. He is a [7]_____ man.
In this picture he is [8]_____ years old.

25 **Match.**

1	bald	**a**	likes speaking a lot
2	handsome	**b**	good-looking for a baby person or animal
3	dark hair	**c**	hair under a man's nose
4	beautiful	**d**	opposite of lazy
5	a mustache	**e**	good at games like soccer and volleyball
6	hard-working	**f**	opposite of light hair
7	creative	**g**	good at art or thinking up new ideas
8	sporty	**h**	good-looking (for women)
9	talkative	**i**	no hair
10	cute	**j**	good-looking (for men)

26 **Write.**

bald   beautiful
blue eyes   good-looking
long hair   spiky hair
straight hair   tall

am/is/are	have/has

27 **Write. Then number.**

1 What _____ she look like? _____ tall and has spiky, black hair.

2 What _____ he look like? _____ short and bald.

3 What _____ they look like? _____ beautiful and have long, straight hair.

28 Unscramble and write questions. Then look at Activity 27 and write the answers.

1 is / like / she / what _____

2 they / like / are / what _____

3 your / like / what / uncle / is _____

29 🎧 09 **Listen and write.**

> bossy   creative   likes   name   smart   spiky   sporty   talkative   tall

My friend

○ What does she look like?

My friend's ¹_____ is Miki. She's ²_____ and

she has short, ³_____ hair. She has brown eyes and she wears

glasses. She ⁴_____ skirts and colorful T-shirts.

○ What's she like?

She's ⁵_____ and ⁶_____. She's a bit

⁷_____ but it's OK. I like her because she's funny,

○ ⁸_____, and ⁹_____.

30 Describe a friend or family member.

What does he/she look like? _____

_____

_____

What's he/she like? _____

_____

_____

⭐ **Are you ready for Unit 2?**

2 My life

1 Number.

a   wash   ☐   b   brush   ☐   c   make   ☐   d   clean   ☐

e   take   ☐   f   meet   ☐   g   do   ☐   h   be   ☐

i   take out   ☐   j   study   ☐

1   the trash   2   my teeth   3   notes in class   4   my face

5   my friends   6   my bed   7   on time   8   my room

9   before a test   10   my homework

2 Look and write. Then listen and ✓ or ✗ for Dan.

		Dan	You
1	I ___ **brush my teeth** ___ in the morning.		
2	I _____ every day.		
3	I'm _____ for school every day.		
4	I _____ in class.		
5	I _____ before a test.		
6	I _____ after school.		
7	I _____ every day.		

3 Look at Activity 2 and ✓ or ✗ for yourself.

4 🎧 **What should they do before bed? Listen and match. Then write.**

1	Robbie and Emma	**a**	brush his teeth
2	Emma	**b**	walk the dog
3	Robbie	**c**	say good night to their parents
4	Dad	**d**	clean the kitchen
5	Mom	**e**	wash her hair

1 _____

2 _____

3 _____

4 _____

5 _____

5 **What should your family do before bed? Write.**

1 I should _____.

2 My _____ should _____.

3 _____

4 _____

6 🎧 **What must they do on Saturday? Listen and match. Then write.**

1	Robbie and Emma	**a**	do homework
2	Mom and Dad	**b**	clean rooms
3	Maddy	**c**	take out the trash
4	Dan	**d**	practice the piano

1 _____

2 _____

7 Write.

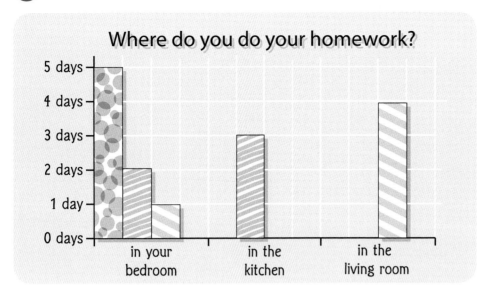

Where do you do your homework?

Matt

Sasha

Jamie

You

1 Matt _____never_____ does his homework in the kitchen.

2 Matt _____ does his homework in his bedroom.

3 Sasha _____ does her homework in her bedroom.

4 Jamie _____ does his homework in the living room.

8 Look at Activity 7 and complete the chart for yourself. Then write.

1 _____ in my bedroom.

2 _____ in the kitchen.

3 _____ in the living room.

9 Find and write.

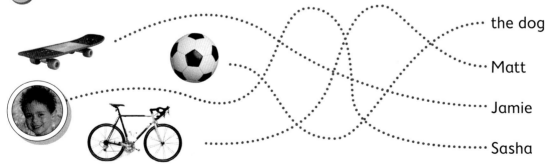

the dog

Matt

Jamie

Sasha

1 This is _____Jamie's_____ skateboard.   **2** _____ ball.

3 _____ brother.   **4** _____ bike.

10   **Listen and check (✓). Then write.**

What does Mira do each day?

MY WEEK	Monday	Tuesday	Wednesday	Thursday	Friday
brush my teeth	✓				
make my bed					
do my homework					
set the table					
take out the trash					

1 <u>She always brushes her teeth.</u> _____

2 _____

3 _____ after dinner.

4 _____

5 _____

11  **Listen and write.**

I ¹_____ get up at ²_____.

I ³_____ leave home at ⁴_____.

I ⁵_____ to school or sometimes run!

I ⁶_____ be on ⁷_____.

School starts at ⁸_____, but I

⁹_____ be there at ¹⁰_____.

Today after school, I ¹¹_____ a birthday

present for my mom. It's her birthday tomorrow.

At home, I ¹²_____ set the table.

Today is Tuesday, so I must take out the trash

¹³_____ bed.

12 Look at the story and write.

STORY

1   Polly and Mike watch _____ working out at the training camp.

2   They hide inside an _____.

3   They make a _____ to keep warm.

4   But then they go to _____!

5   Smith leaves his _____ at the training camp.

6   The red ribbons are the same as the ribbons in the _____.

13 Look and write.

> cleans his room   goes to bed   eats dinner
> ~~eats lunch~~   washes the dog   watches TV

1

He eats lunch at
twelve-thirty.

2

_____
_____

3

_____
_____

4

_____
_____

5

_____
_____

6

_____
_____

14 Imagine. What happens next in the story?

I think _____.

15 Number. Then write.

What should Sarah give each friend?

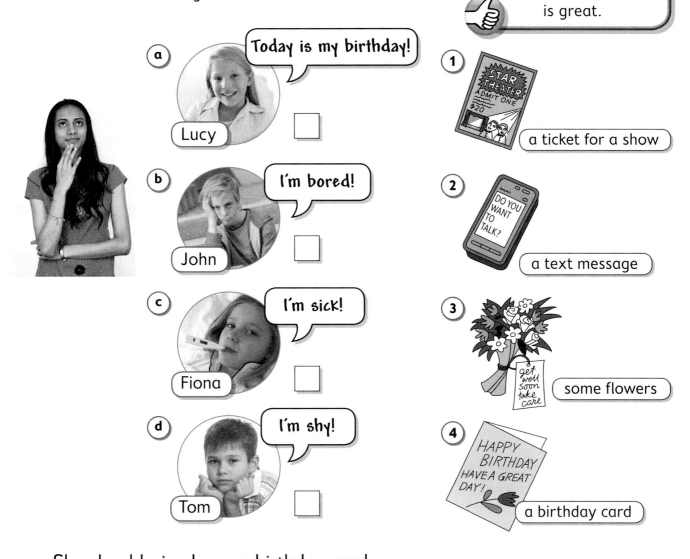

a Lucy — Today is my birthday!
b John — I'm bored!
c Fiona — I'm sick!
d Tom — I'm shy!

1 a ticket for a show
2 a text message
3 some flowers
4 a birthday card

a <u>She should give Lucy a birthday card.</u>

b _____

c _____

d _____

16 Think of two people you know (family or friends). What are they like? What should you give them? Write.

1 I should give _____.

2 _____

17 **Write.**

1 He _____goes_____ (go) to school.

   He ____must go____ (go + must) to school.

2 She _____ (watch) TV.

   She _____ (watch + should + not) TV all day.

3 He _____ (make) his bed.

   He _____ (make + should) his bed.

4 She _____ (wash) her face.

   She _____ (wash + should) her face before school.

5 He _____ (do) his homework.

   He _____ (do + must) his homework.

6 She _____ (brush) her hair.

   She _____ (brush + should) her hair.

18 **Look and write.**

> always   always eats   his   must get up   often eat
> should   sometimes sings   usually get up

I don't like mornings. My big brother ¹_____ gets up at five

o'clock. He ²_____ early every day because he's a farmer.

He ³_____ songs in the morning. ⁴_____ songs are

horrible. I can't sleep after that. I ⁵_____ at six o'clock because

I'm hungry. I like eggs for breakfast but I ⁶_____ toast. Why?

Because my brother ⁷_____ all of our eggs at 5:30.

He ⁸_____ give me some but he doesn't. Grrr!

19 Read and choose ✓ or ✗. Then find and write the hidden word.

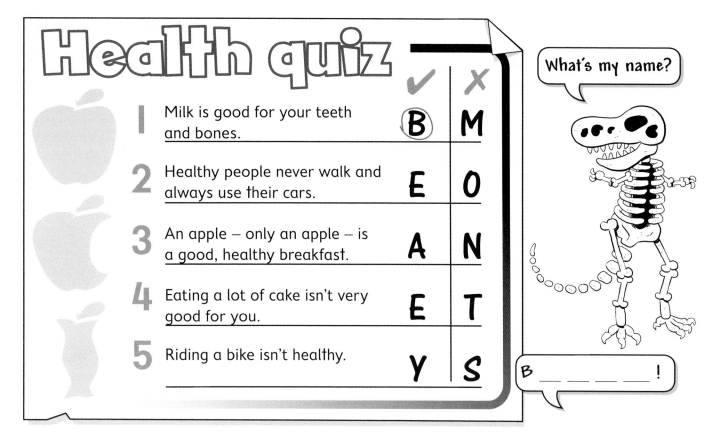

Health quiz

		✓	✗
1	Milk is good for your teeth and bones.	(B)	M
2	Healthy people never walk and always use their cars.	E	O
3	An apple – only an apple – is a good, healthy breakfast.	A	N
4	Eating a lot of cake isn't very good for you.	E	T
5	Riding a bike isn't healthy.	Y	S

What's my name?

B _ _ _ _ _ _ !

20 Read. Then listen and correct six differences. Then circle.

Application form

We are looking for healthy soccer players for our soccer team. Write about your day.

ten

I get up at ~~seven~~ o'clock. I have eggs on toast for breakfast. I always brush

my teeth after breakfast. I often play soccer in the afternoon. After that,

I take a shower, eat dinner, and I go to bed at nine o'clock.

Do you think he is a healthy person?   (Yes / No)

21 Match.

1	be on time	**a**	make something not dirty
2	homework	**b**	use water and a toothbrush
3	trash	**c**	listen and write
4	take notes	**d**	schoolwork to do after school finishes
5	clean	**e**	use water and soap
6	brush my teeth	**f**	opposite of always
7	wash my face	**g**	not early and not late
8	never	**h**	things you don't want
9	study before a test	**i**	maybe four times a week
10	often	**j**	You must do this a lot to get 100%.

22 Unscramble and write. Then number.

1 day / every / must / you / make / your / bed

_____

2 after / brush / breakfast / teeth / should / they / their

_____

3 help / the / parents / should / we / our / clean / house

_____

4 this / 10 p.m. / homework / must / I / finish / before

_____

23 Look at Activity 22 and number to match the answers.

1 We sometimes help our mom and dad in the house.

2 Because I should go to bed at ten.

3 I always make my bed. I never forget.

4 They usually brush their teeth then and they always brush them before bed.

24   **Listen and write.**

> always   dinner   help   must   often   should   sometimes   wash

My evenings

In the evening, I ¹_____ do my homework. I ²_____
do my homework before ³_____. After dinner, I ⁴_____
my mom clean the table and ⁵_____ the dishes. I ⁶_____
watch TV at 7:30 because my favorite show is on from 7:30 to 8:00.
I ⁷_____ email friends or play on my computer. I ⁸_____
go to bed at 10:00, but sometimes I'm late.

25 **Describe a friend or family member.**

_____
_____
_____
_____
_____
_____
_____
_____
_____
_____
_____

 Are you ready for Unit 3?

3 Free time

1 Match.

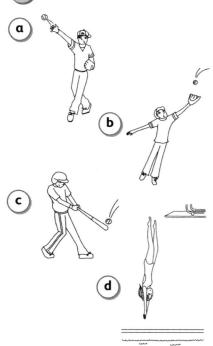

1 going shopping
2 throwing
3 hitting
4 catching
5 diving
6 kicking
7 telling jokes
8 jumping on the trampoline
9 reading poetry

2 Look and write.

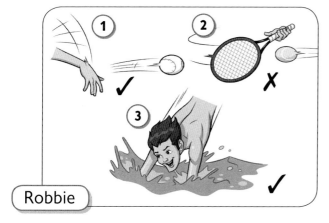

Robbie

Dan

1 I'm good at _____throwing_____ .

2 I'm not good at _____ .

3 I'm _____ .

4 I'm _____ .

5 I'm _____ .

6 I'm _____ .

3 Look at Activity 2 and listen. Who is talking – Robbie or Dan?

4 Look and write.

1 ¹ _____ are you good at?

² _____ good ³ _____ throwing.

2 He ⁴ _____ good at catching.

Are ⁵ _____ good at running?

3 ⁶ _____ you ⁷ _____ at climbing?

4 Yes, I ⁸ _____ , but ⁹ _____ good at jumping!

5 Write questions. Then circle for yourself.

1 <u>Are you good at kicking?</u>   (Yes, I am. / No, I'm not.)

2 _____ (Yes, I am. / No, I'm not.)

3 _____ (Yes, I am. / No, I'm not.)

4 _____ (Yes, I am. / No, I'm not.)

6 Write about your friends.

1 (likes) _____

2 (loves) _____

7 Complete the crossword. Then find, write, and circle.

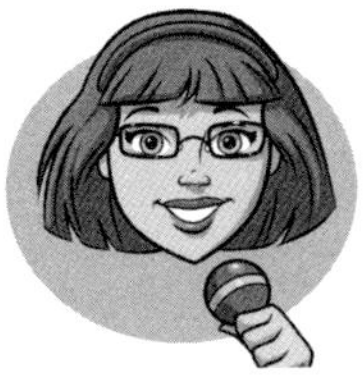

I love ___ ___ ___ ___ ___ ___ ___ ___ ___ (at the beach! / Karaoke! / in a pool)!

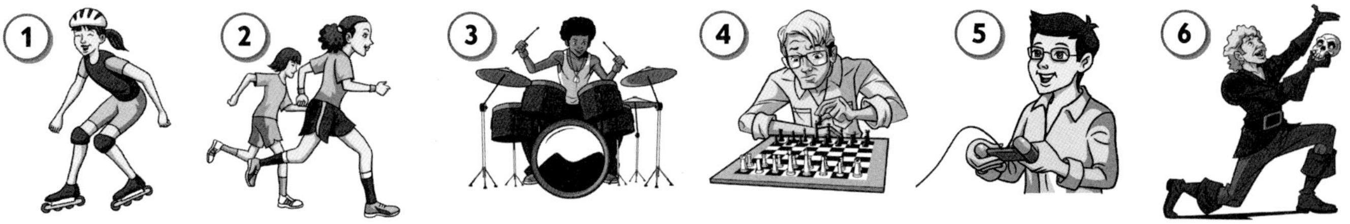

1   2   3   4   5   6

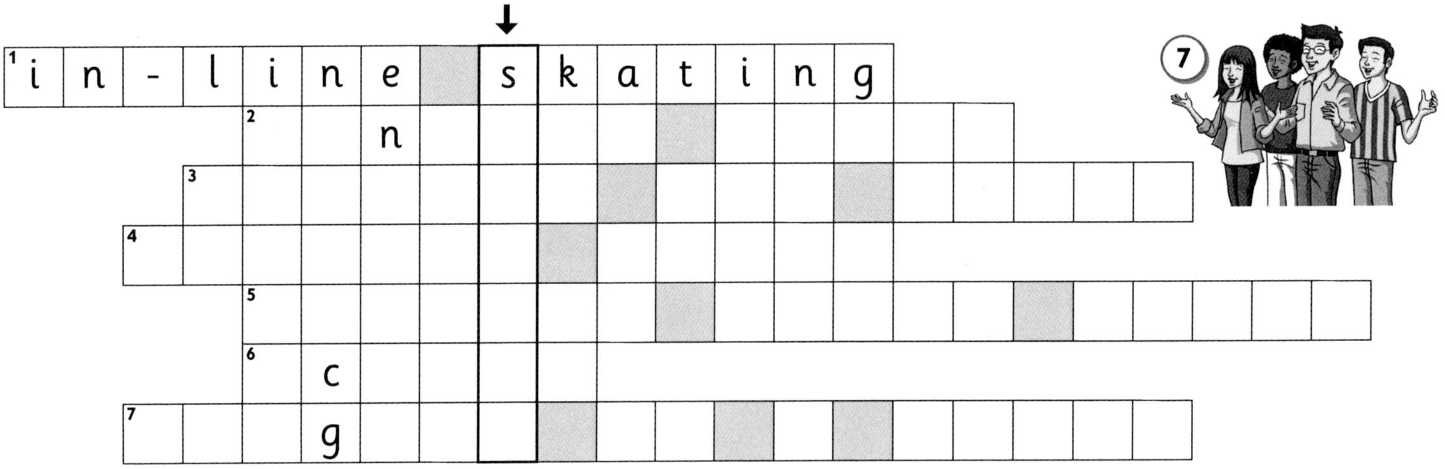

↓

¹i	n	-	l	i	n	e		s	k	a	t	i	n	g			
			²		n												
	³															
⁴															
	⁵														
	⁶	c													
⁷		g													

7

8 Look and write.

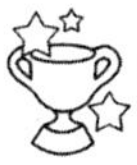

🏆 = is/are good at   💗 = loves/love   😣 = doesn't/don't like

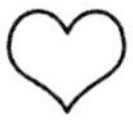

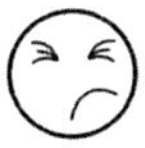

1 _____

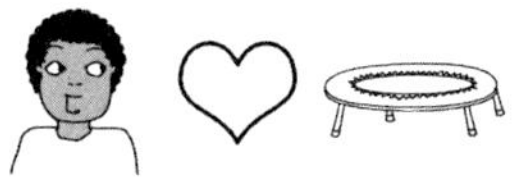

2 _____

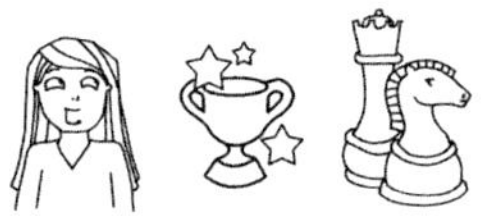

3 _____

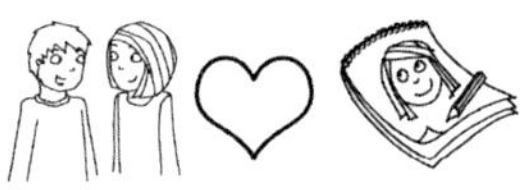

4 _____

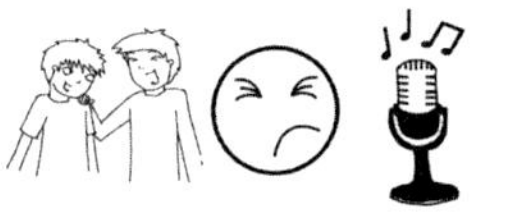

5 _____

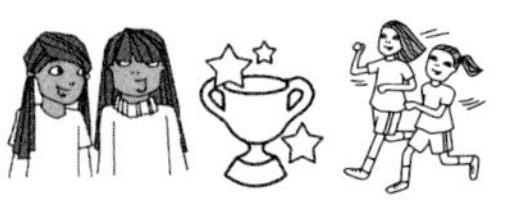

6 _____

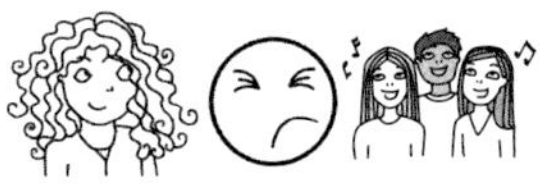

9 Write.

YESTERDAY	Robbie	Emma	Maddy and Dan
7:00	sleeping	eating breakfast	walking to school
11:00	studying music	writing a story	swimming
12:00	eating lunch	eating lunch	playing with friends
2:45	having computer class	drawing in class	reading in English class
5:00	playing soccer at school	working on a project	eating ice cream with friends
8:00	singing in the bathtub	meeting friends	watching TV

1   What was Robbie doing yesterday at 7:00? He was _____.

2   What _____ Maddy and Dan doing yesterday at 11:00?

    They were _____.

3   What _____ Emma doing yesterday at 12:00?

    She _____ lunch.

4   What _____ Maddy and Dan doing yesterday at 2:45?

    They _____ in English class.

5   What _____ Robbie _____ yesterday at _____?

    _____ soccer at school.

6   What _____ Emma _____ yesterday at 8:00?

    _____

10 Write. Then look at Activity 9 and circle.

1   Was Emma eating breakfast at 7:00? (Yes, she _____. / No, she wasn't.)

2   _____ Maddy and Dan _____ lunch at 12:00?

    (Yes, they _____. / No, they _____.)

3   _____ Robbie _____ on a project at 2:45?

    (Yes, he was. / No, _____.)

4   _____ Maddy and Dan _____ TV at 8:00?

    (Yes, _____. / No, _____.)

11 **Look at the story and circle T = True or F = False. Correct the false sentences.**

1 Polly wants to go towards the town.

T / F _____

2 Mike's mom made them breakfast.

T / F _____

3 The skidoo woke Polly up at 2:00 a.m.

T / F _____

4 Mike always plays soccer on Sundays.

T / F _____

5 They see tracks, the roof of Bollington Hall, and red wolves.

T / F _____

12 **Read and write.**

1

Are they good at _____?

Yes, they are.

2

Is he good at diving?

_____

3

Does he love _____?

_____

4

_____

No, they aren't.

13 **Imagine. What happens next in the story?**

I think _____.

14 Write your advice.

join a drama club   join a sports team
~~learn computer programming~~
start a band   take art classes

1  I like computers but I'm not good at playing video games.

He should learn computer programming. _____

2  I love acting and dancing.

_____

3  We like drawing. We love making things.

_____

4  I'm very good at P.E. I love doing headstands!

_____

5  I'm good at playing the guitar. I love singing.

_____

15 Think of two friends or family members. Suggest hobbies and explain why.

1 My brother should start a band because he's good at singing and playing the drums.

2 _____

_____

16   **Read. Then listen and correct six differences.**

Dear Grandma,

Action Camp is great! I'm here with Ellie because we both love sports. We go swimming every

morning. I love ~~sleeping~~. I can swim 50 meters underwater now. We have dance lessons, too. I'm
      swimming

not very good at diving because I feel scared, but Ellie can dive from the big diving board. She's

fantastic! Ellie and I like jumping on the trampoline after breakfast and we love playing soccer

together in the morning. Ellie is very good at running and hitting the ball.

Mark

17 **Look at Activity 16 and write.**

1 What does Mark love doing in the morning? _____

2 Can Mark swim? _____

3 Is Mark good at diving? _____

4 Is Ellie good at diving? _____

5 What do Ellie and Mark like doing after lunch? _____

6 Do they like playing tennis? _____

18 **Write the -*ing* form.**

+ ing			**+ last letter + ing**			**- e + ing**	
kick	**kicking**		swim	**swimming**		dance	**dancing**
sing	_____		hit	_____		dive	_____
play	_____		run	_____		ride	_____

19 Write.

good at   my   play   playing   write   writing

Hi. ¹_____ name's David. I have guitar lessons every week. I love ²_____ the guitar – my teacher is great. My friend, Melissa, is ³_____ singing and her brother can ⁴_____ the drums. Last Sunday, we were playing songs all day. It was fun! I like ⁵_____ music, too. One day, I want to ⁶_____ music for movies.

20 Listen to the music and check (✓) for yourself.

1	cool ☐	OK ☐	bad ☐	2	cool ☐	OK ☐	bad ☐
3	cool ☐	OK ☐	bad ☐	4	cool ☐	OK ☐	bad ☐
5	cool ☐	OK ☐	bad ☐	6	cool ☐	OK ☐	bad ☐
7	cool ☐	OK ☐	bad ☐	8	cool ☐	OK ☐	bad ☐

21 Listen again and choose your favorite. Then find that number and read about yourself.

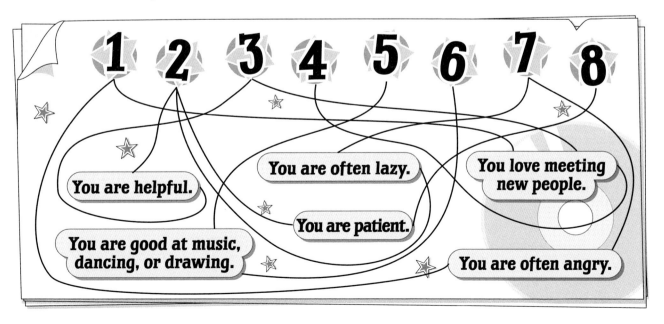

1 2 3 4 5 6 7 8

You are helpful.

You are often lazy.

You love meeting new people.

You are patient.

You are good at music, dancing, or drawing.

You are often angry.

22 Match.

1	poetry	a	an old, popular game for two players
2	a joke	b	a jumping sport
3	video game	c	This is a group musical performance of a song.
4	diving	d	a type of writing; the words sometimes sound the same
5	shopping	e	reading and singing along to music
6	chess	f	buying things
7	jumping on the trampoline	g	You can play this on a TV.
8	karaoke	h	jumping fingers first into a swimming pool
9	acting	i	This should be funny.
10	singing in a choir	j	speaking and doing actions on a stage

23 Write. Then listen and circle T = True or F = False.

1 Sam ♡ 🎸

_____ T / F

2 Anna ✗ ♟

_____ T / F

3 The children 🏆 🎤

_____ T / F

4 Bill 😠 🎨

_____ T / F

🏆 = is/are good at
♡ = loves/love
✗ = can't
😠 = doesn't/don't like

24 Write the missing word. Then write the answer.

1 What _____ she doing yesterday?

_____

2 What _____ they doing yesterday?

_____

25  **Listen and write.**

My activities

I like ¹_____ tennis. I play tennis at a club. Yesterday, I ²_____ playing in the afternoon. We usually play games on Sunday and we ³_____ on Wednesday. I love swimming, too. I ⁴_____ swimming on Monday and Thursday. I ⁵_____ swimming in the ocean ⁶_____ the summer, too. At school, I'm ⁷_____ at sports and English. I'm ⁸_____ good at art ⁹_____ the teacher helps me a lot.

26 **Write about things you like, don't like, and things you can do.**

_____

_____

_____

_____

_____

_____

_____

_____

_____

_____

_____

_____

 Are you ready for Unit 4?

4 Around the world

1 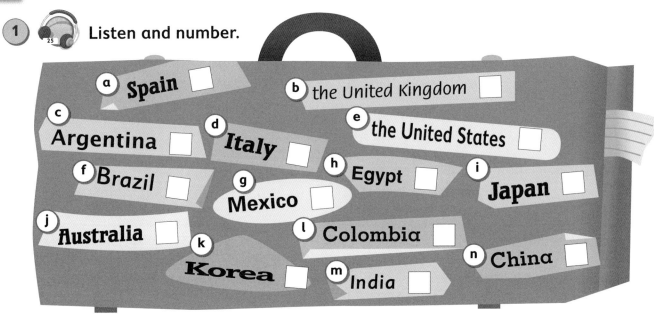 Listen and number.

a) **Spain** ☐
b) the United Kingdom ☐
c) Argentina ☐
d) **Italy** ☐
e) the United States ☐
f) Brazil ☐
g) Mexico ☐
h) Egypt ☐
i) **Japan** ☐
j) **Australia** ☐
k) **Korea** ☐
l) Colombia ☐
m) India ☐
n) China ☐

2 Complete the crossword. Use the words from Activity 1.

4. T H E U N I T E D S T A T E S

3 Look and write.

1 <u>There's</u> an old man under _____ .

2 _____ two birds _____ umbrella.

3 _____ an umbrella on _____ .

4 _____ cats on the _____ .

5 _____ monkeys in the ocean.

4 Read and write *a*, *some*, or *any*.

1 There are _____ long rivers in the United States.

2 There isn't _____ rain forest in Italy.

3 There aren't _____ giraffes in the United Kingdom.

4 There are _____ old houses in Spain.

5 There's _____ big waterfall in Brazil and Argentina.

5 Write.

1 hippos / China / ✗ _____

2 a rain forest / Australia / ✓ _____

3 a snowy mountain / Egypt / ✗ _____

4 elephants / Mexico / ✗ _____

5 beautiful beaches / Spain / ✓ _____

6 Write three things about your country.

1 _____ .

2 _____ .

3 _____ .

7 Find and circle nine words. Then find and write the answer using the letters that aren't circled.

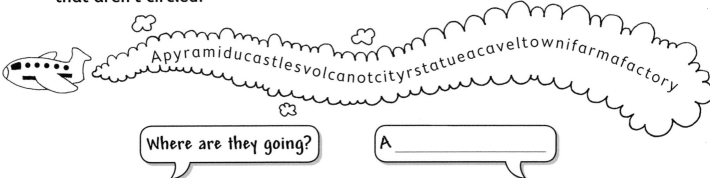

Apyramiducastlesvolcanotcityrstatueacaveltownifarmafactory

Where are they going?

A _____

8 Look and write. Use words from Activity 7.

			The United Kingdom	Spain
1		a _____	✓	✓
2		_____es	✗	✓
3		a _____	✓	✓
4		_____s	✓	✓
5		_____s	✗	✗
6		_____s	✓	✓
7		a _____	✓	✓
8		_____ies	✓	✓
9		a _____	✓	✓

9 Look at Activity 8 and write.

1 _____ pyramids _____ Spain?

No, there aren't. _____

2 _____ castle _____ Spain?

_____

3 _____ volcanoes _____ the United Kingdom?

_____

4 _____ caves _____ the United Kingdom?

_____

10 Read, guess, and write. Then listen and check your answers.

1 Are there any beaches in Australia? Yes, there are. _____

2 Is there a rain forest in Korea? _____

3 Are there any volcanoes in Italy? _____

4 Are there any volcanoes in Mexico? _____

5 Is there a mountain taller than 5,000 meters in Japan? _____

6 Is there a river longer than the Amazon in China? _____

11 Write your own quiz.

1 Are there any pyramids in Argentina? _____

No, there aren't. _____

2 _____

_____

3 _____

_____

12 **Look at the story and correct the sentences.**

1   Hector Frost has a map.

_____

2   There aren't any roads to the research station.

_____

3   There are some tracks going towards town.

_____

4   There aren't any ribbons on the dog.

_____

5   Frost is happy to see the children in the forest.

_____

13   **Listen and circle the correct dog. Then write.**

The dog is _____
_____.

_____
_____

_____
_____

14 **Imagine. What happens next in the story?**

I think _____.

15 Choose two teams for an English project.
The people should be good at different things.

4

I can draw.

I'm good at using computers and the Internet.

Peter

I'm good at writing.

Sofia

I'm friendly and talkative.

Sandra

I like finding things on the Internet.

I'm good at painting.

Jenny

Maria

I like working with people.

George

John

I love reading and writing.

Diego

Skill	Writing	Art	Computers	Talking
Team A				
Team B				

16 What can you give to a team? Write.

I'm good at _____.

I like _____.

I'm not good at _____.

I don't like _____.

17   **Listen and circle.**

1 Mia is in (Brazil / Mexico).

2 Mia is talking to her (grandma / grandpa).

3 Mia is in a (rain forest / city).

4 There are some (beaches / pyramids) in Rio de Janeiro.

5 There's a big (volcano / statue), too.

6 A lot of people in Brazil are good at (dancing / singing).

18 **Write.**

animals   beautiful   Grandpa   rain forest   river   trees

Dear ¹_____,

Hello from the Amazon ²_____ in Brazil!
There are a lot of tall green ³_____ in the
rain forest and some scary ⁴_____,
too! I'm fishing in a ⁵_____ today. I can see
some monkeys! It's very ⁶_____ here.

See you soon!

Mia

19 **Imagine you're on vacation. Write to a friend.**

Hi _____,

I'm in _____.

There are some _____

_____.

There aren't any _____

_____.

20 **Listen and write.**

Come to Greenland!

¹ _____ on skidoos!

Climb snowy ² _____!

See ³ _____ and waterfalls of ice! There aren't ⁴ _____ big cities here but there are ⁵ _____ beautiful polar ⁶ _____ and reindeer in this cold place. Every ⁷ _____ in Greenland is an adventure!

Greenland – a world of ice!

21 **Check (✓) for you.**

Is a vacation in Greenland right for you?

1 I like doing sports:

A on snow, ice, and water. ☐

B on grass. ☐

2 I like eating:

A meat and fish. ☐

B fruit. ☐

3 My favorite clothes are:

A a warm coat and a hat. ☐

B shorts and a T-shirt. ☐

4 In my bedroom, there are some pictures of:

A animals. ☐

B famous people. ☐

5 My favorite time of year is:

A winter. ☐

B summer. ☐

a lot of **A**s: Go to Greenland. It's a great place for you. a lot of **B**s: Don't go to Greenland. Choose a warm place for your vacation.

22 Match.

1	a volcano	**a**	There are some famous ones in Egypt; people made them a long time ago.
2	rain forest		
3	beach	**b**	a country in North America
4	pyramids	**c**	the sand next to the ocean
5	city	**d**	This is an area with lots of trees that has lots of wet weather.
6	Argentina	**e**	There are animals, fruit, and vegetables in this place.
7	Korea	**f**	a country in South America
8	the United States	**g**	People work here and make things.
9	factory	**h**	A lot of people live here – it's bigger than a town.
10	farm	**i**	a country in Asia
		j	Hot liquid sometimes comes out of this type of mountain.

23 Unscramble and write questions. Then write the answers.

1 there / is / desert / in / Asia / a

_____

(✓) _____

2 is / rain forest / there / a / Italy / in

_____

(✗) _____

3 are / statues / in / Brazil / there / any

_____

(✓) _____

4 volcanoes / are / there / in / any / Egypt

_____

(✓) _____

24   **Listen and write.**

The river

There's a river near my house. I go there ¹_____ my bike.

²_____ aren't ³_____ people near the river.

There ⁴_____ a lot of trees and ⁵_____ . The birds

⁶_____ in the trees. There are ⁷_____ in the river and

⁸_____ they jump. ⁹_____ a bridge over the river.

Sometimes, I sit ¹⁰_____ the bridge and read. I love the river.

25 **Write about a place you know.**

_____

_____

_____

_____

_____

_____

_____

_____

_____

_____

_____

_____

 Are you ready for Unit 5?

5 Shopping

1 Find and circle.

1
2
3
4
5

b	r	a	c	e	l	e	t	m	w
i	s	h	y	r	e	x	f	b	h
s	u	n	g	l	a	s	s	e	s
j	m	k	l	q	m	l	a	l	w
j	b	t	o	d	b	l	v	t	i
a	r	f	v	a	z	p	n	a	m
c	e	j	e	w	a	t	c	h	s
k	l	c	s	b	u	n	p	o	u
e	l	g	w	a	l	l	e	t	i
t	a	h	a	n	d	b	a	g	t
m	o	x	y	h	o	o	d	i	e

6
7
8
9
10
11

2 Write. Use *is* or *are* and words from Activity 1.

1
How much _____
that _____?

2
How much _____
those _____?

3
How much _____
that _____?

4
How much _____
those _____?

3 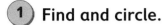 Listen. What does Maddy buy?

4 Look and write the prices in words.

1 _____

2 _____

3 _____

4 _____

5 _____

6 _____

5 The prices in Activity 4 are wrong. Listen and circle the correct prices.

1	**a** $28	**b** $29.90	**c** $29		**2**	**a** $12.50	**b** $20.50	**c** $15.20
3	**a** $9	**b** $19	**c** $90		**4**	**a** $212	**b** $200	**c** $121
5	**a** $40.20	**b** $42.20	**c** $42		**6**	**a** $26.50	**b** $25.50	**c** $25.55

6 Write.

course   dollars   how   hundred   much   please

David: Hello. How ¹_____ are those gloves, please?

Store clerk: They're four ²_____ and fifty cents.

David: And ³_____ much is that watch?

Store clerk: It's one ⁴_____ dollars.

David: Oh... may I buy the gloves, ⁵_____?

Store clerk: Yes, of ⁶_____.

Lesson 2

49

7 Number.

a a cheap bracelet ☐

b an old-fashioned watch ☐

c a modern watch ☐

d an expensive bracelet ☐

e baggy jeans ☐

f a tight sweater ☐

① ② $2 ③ ④ $199 ⑤ ⑥

8 Write. Use words from Activity 7.

①

These pants are too _____.

②

That _____.

③

This _____.

④

These _____.

9 Write sentences.

baggy big dark light long old
old-fashioned short small tight

My green sweater is too tight.

1 _____

2 _____

10 **Match the opposites.**

1	expensive	**a**	baggy
2	modern	**b**	long
3	tight	**c**	old-fashioned
4	big	**d**	cheap
5	short	**e**	small

11 **Write.**

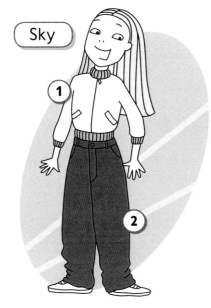

Sky

Lee

1 <u>That jacket is too short.</u>
_____ (short)

3 _____
_____ (tight)

2 _____
_____ (baggy)

4 _____
_____ (long)

12 **Look at Activity 11 and write.**

1 Whose jacket is this? _____. It's hers.

2 Whose pants are these? _____. They're _____.

3 _____? It's Lee's. It's _____.

4 _____? They're Lee's. _____.

13 **Look at the story and write.**

1 Who is helping the explorers in the store? _____

2 What costs 500 Ice dollars? _____

3 Who wants to go to the lake? _____

4 Who is hiding near the lake? _____

5 Who does Smith push into the lake? _____

6 Does Gizmo catch Smith? _____

14 **Listen and write the prices. What does the Queen buy?**

1 $9.99 _____ **2** _____ **3** _____

4 _____ **5** _____ **6** _____

15 **Imagine. What happens next in the story?**

I think _____.

16 What should they wear? Read and ✓ or ✗.

VALUES

👍 Dress correctly for each occasion.

5

1 I have a wedding this evening.

2 I have a party tonight.

3 I am going walking in the mountains.

a light blue dress ☐
blue sneakers ☐
a white belt ☐
a light blue cap ☐
white shoes ☐
sunglasses ☐
a dark blue hat ☐
a gold bracelet ☐
a swimsuit ☐

baggy pants ☐
jeans ☐
a white shirt ☐
a dark green jacket ☐
a red belt ☐
black sneakers ☐
shorts ☐
a black T-shirt ☐
sunglasses ☐

tight jeans ☐
a baggy T-shirt ☐
sunglasses ☐
a warm jacket ☐
a yellow scarf ☐
sneakers ☐
baggy shorts ☐
a cap ☐
boots ☐

17 What do you wear to a wedding or a school party? Write.

A wedding
1 _____
2 _____
3 _____
4 _____

A school party
1 _____
2 _____
3 _____
4 _____

18 **Listen and check (✓) the ads the boys talk about.**

¹ **BIKE**, blue, $123,
for a boy 160 cm tall.
Tel: 555-9751 ☐

² **VIDEO GAMES**,
20 games for $17.
gamecity@yoohoo.com ☐

³ **SCARF**, $6.50, red and white.
soccerfan@bkinternet.com ☐

⁴ **SKATEBOARD**, new, $38.
Tel: 555-3184 ☐

⁵ **JACKET**, $25, white, for a four-year-old girl.
whiteshop@compuworld.com ☐

19 **Listen again and circle.**

1   The bike in the ad is too (big / expensive / small).

2   The skateboard is too (expensive / big / old-fashioned).

3   Tom wants to buy the (skateboard / video games / bike).

20 Draw three things. Then write ads for them.

21 Write.

> a hat   a jacket   a swimsuit   shorts and a T-shirt   sunglasses

Clothes list for sailing lessons

1 _____

You will get hot. Don't wear long pants or long sleeves.

2 _____

At sea, the weather can change quickly. It's often windy, even on sunny days.

3 _____

The sunlight on the water is very bad for your eyes.

4 _____

You should cover your head from the sun.

5 _____

After the lessons, you can dive from the boat and have fun in the water. But take off your sailing shoes first!

22 **Listen and write.**

		Activity	Clothes
1	Jack	1 _____	warm 2 _____ 3 _____ 4 _____
2	Pete	5 _____ class	6 _____ shoes 7 _____ 8 _____ pants
3	Sally	9 _____ riding	long 10 _____ 11 _____ pants hard 12 _____

23 Match.

1	umbrella	a	opposite of baggy
2	bracelet	b	You can keep your money and cell phone in here.
3	wallet	c	You can use this on rainy days.
4	handbag	d	opposite of dark
5	short	e	You can keep your money in this.
6	tight	f	opposite of long
7	light	g	You can wear one or more of these on your arm.

24 Number to make a dialog.

a Oh! That's too expensive. I only have twenty dollars.
How much are those dark blue jeans?

b Yes, of course. Eight dollars, please.

c Great. May I buy it, please?

d They're eighteen dollars and fifty cents.

e Well, they're cheap, but they're too baggy.
I like wearing tight jeans. How much is that scarf?

f The sweater is twenty-one dollars.

g Excuse me. How much is that sweater?

h It's eight dollars.

25 Listen and write. Whose are these?

1   2   3   4

_____   _____   _____   _____

26 **Listen and write.**

My clothes

My favorite [1]_____ is white with small letters on the

[2]_____. It's really cool. My favorite shoes are my

[3]_____. They're [4]_____ and black. I don't like my

winter boots [5]_____ they're [6]_____ and my summer

[7]_____ are [8]_____ small now. I like my

[9]_____ uniform. I really like the jacket. It's green and gold. They're

my favorite [10]_____.

27 **Write about your clothes.**

_____

_____

_____

_____

_____

_____

_____

_____

_____

_____

_____

_____

 Are you ready for Unit 6?

6 Party time

1 Write.

		Yesterday,...
1	make	I _____ a sandwich for lunch.
2	have	I _____ dinner at 6:00 p.m.
3	come	I _____ to school by bus.
4	give	I _____ my friend a present.
5	see	I _____ my grandma.
6	bring	I _____ my lunch to school.
7	meet	I _____ my grandpa.
8	eat	I _____ curry.
9	get	I _____ 100% on a test.
10	sing	I _____ in a choir.

2 Write.

1 Yesterday _____ Dan's birthday. He is 12 now.

2 He _____ a new soccer ball.

3 Robbie _____ Dan some sneakers for a present.

4 The party was fun. Everyone _____ "Happy Birthday."

5 Dan's cousins _____ to the party.

6 There _____ some games in the garden.

7 They _____ pizza and cake after the games.

8 Dan's mom _____ the birthday cake.

3 Listen and check (✓) the true sentences in Activity 2.

4 Write.

Robbie [1]_____ a birthday party in February. A lot of friends [2]_____ to the party. They [3]_____ food, drinks, and presents. Dan [4]_____ Robbie a wallet for his birthday. Emma didn't bring a present because she [5]_____ a very big cake for Robbie.

Robbie's party

5 Write.

Emma had a birthday party in July. Maddy came, but Kipper didn't [1]_____. Robbie brought a small cake from a store. He's not good at cooking so he didn't [2]_____ it. They didn't [3]_____ songs but there was music so everyone danced. There were sandwiches but they didn't [4]_____ a lot of drinks.

Emma's party

6 Look at the two pictures above and check (✓) Robbie or Emma.

		Robbie	Emma
1	It was sunny.	☐	☐
2	Friends played music but didn't sing.	☐	☐
3	There was a big cake.	☐	☐
4	Maddy didn't come to the party.	☐	☐
5	Seven children came to the party.	☐	☐
6	They had a lot of drinks.	☐	☐

7 Listen and match.

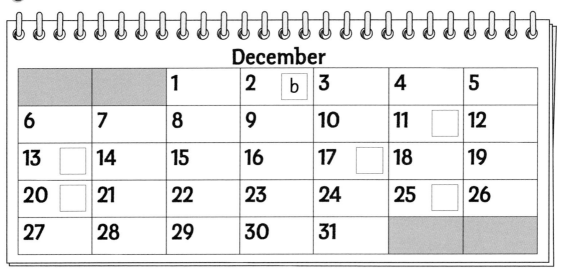

December

		1	2 [b]	3	4	5
6	7	8	9	10	11 ☐	12
13 ☐	14	15	16	17 ☐	18	19
20 ☐	21	22	23	24	25 ☐	26
27	28	29	30	31		

a Christmas

b Taylor's BIRTHDAY

c Mom's Birthday

d Party at School

e Soccer Club Party

f Dance Show

8 Write the dates from Activity 7.

1 Annabel went to a party at school on _____ December 20th _____.

2 She had a big meal with her family for Christmas on _____.

3 She sang "Happy Birthday!" to her mom on _____.

4 She sang "Happy Birthday!" to her cousin on _____.

5 She went to her soccer club party on _____.

6 She went to a dance show on _____.

9 Write about something you did last month. What did you do and when did you do it?

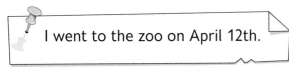

I went to the zoo on April 12th.

_____

_____

10 Listen and write the dates.

Place	Date	Activities
China	July _____	go on a boat; see a lot of tall buildings
	July _____	walk on the Great Wall of China
Korea	July _____	meet some new friends; have a party
	July _____	go to an island; play on a beach
Japan	July _____	see a temple; eat a lot of fish
	July _____	go on a fast train; climb Mount Fuji

11 Look at Activity 10 and write.

1 On July _____, they went to _____. They _____ on a boat and _____ a lot of tall buildings.

2 On July _____, they _____ on the Great Wall of China.

3 On July _____, they went to _____. They _____ some new friends and _____ a party.

4 On July _____, they went to an island and _____ on a beach.

5 On July _____, they went to _____. They _____ a temple and _____ a lot of fish.

6 On July _____, they went on a fast train and _____ Mount Fuji.

12 Look at the story and number the sentences in order.

STORY

a   They gave the red ribbon and the logo to the Police Chief. ☐

b   The Police Chief said, "Come on, let's go." ☐

c   Smith ran to Bollington Hall. ☐

d   Polly and Mike went to the police station. ☐

e   The Police Chief told them about Hector Frost. ☐

f   Smith said, "The kids ran away." ☐

13 Read and draw.

There was a lake near a mountain. It was snowy. There were some trees on the mountain. There was ice over the lake. There were two explorers fishing in a hole in the ice. There was a red bag behind them. It was empty. There was a polar bear on one side of the bag. It had a fish in its mouth. There was a wolf on the other side of the bag. It also wanted the fish!

14 Imagine. What happens next in Mike and Polly's story?

I think _____.

15 Match.

Problems

1 I have a sailing lesson. What should I wear?

2 I don't know the meaning of a word.

3 I'm not good at writing.

4 I don't have money to buy a birthday present.

5 I want to play soccer. I'm not good at it.

6 I have a test and feel nervous.

7 I can't remember vocabulary easily.

Solutions

a Write about things you like.

b Make lists of new words.

c Wear old jeans, a T-shirt, and a warm jacket.

d Don't worry. Make a birthday card.

e Use a dictionary.

f Invite a friend to study with you.

g Don't worry. Play for fun.

16 Think and write other solutions to the problems in Activity 15.

Problem 1: _____

Problem 2: _____

Problem 3: _____

Problem 4: _____

Problem 5: _____

Problem 6: _____

Problem 7: _____

17 Write about a problem you had before and how you solved it.

Problem: _____

Solution: _____

18 **Listen and number.**

a

b

c

d

19 **Listen again and complete for Lucy.**

	Lucy	You
Where was the party?	the ¹ _____beach_____	
How was the weather?	² _____ but ³ _____	
What food was there?	⁴ _____, salad, and strawberries	
What games were there?	⁵ _____	
Did you dance?	⁶ _____, we _____.	
Did you sing?	⁷ _____, we _____.	

20 Imagine you went to a party. Complete the table in Activity 19 for yourself. Then write full sentences below.

> The party was at the beach. The weather was sunny but windy.

_____

_____

21 Listen and check (✓) the things that were on the *Mayflower*.

a doctor ☐   horses ☐   a teacher ☐   hats ☐

chickens ☐   books ☐   cows ☐   clothes ☐

pigs ☐   beds ☐

22 Write.

My Journal, by Samuel Payne

December 22nd, 1661

Our first months here ¹_____ (be) very bad. My parents ²_____
(be) very thin because there was no food. I ³_____ (be) thin, too. We were
very scared.

In the summer, I often ⁴_____ (go) to the river with my Native American friends.
I ⁵_____ (be) good at fishing! Then, in the fall, we ⁶_____ (have) a
big Thanksgiving party. We ⁷_____ (eat) good food and ⁸_____ (say)
thank you to the Native Americans for their help.

23 Write the end of Samuel's journal in Activity 22. Use the words in the box.

50 settlers   fish from the river   meat
songs and games   vegetables from our farm

At the party there were 90 Native Americans and _____

_____

_____

_____

_____

24 Write the missing words.

1	first	→	second	→	third	→	_____
2	first	→	third	→	fifth	→	_____
3	tenth	→	fifteenth	→	twentieth	→	_____
4	third	→	tenth	→	seventeenth	→	_____
5	first	→	_____	→	twenty-first	→	thirty-first
6	thirteenth	→	tenth	→	_____	→	fourth
7	twenty-fourth	→	twelfth	→	_____	→	third
8	_____	→	fourth	→	eighth	→	sixteenth

25 Write about what you did last week.

1   (come)   <u>Last week, I came home from school early every day.</u>

2   (give)   _____

3   (see)   _____

4   (eat)   _____

5   (get)   _____

6   (go)   _____

26 Circle.

Yesterday, I ¹(went / brought) to a birthday party. I ²(made / met) some old friends and ³(make / made) many new friends at the party. The party was in my town's park. We ⁴(had / have) lots of food and drink and ⁵(played / play) lots of games. We didn't ⁶(bring / brought) the food but we ⁷(ate / eat) it! We ⁸(was / were) very tired after the party but it ⁹(was / were) a fantastic day.

27 Look at Activity 26 and write.

1   When was the birthday party? _____

2   Where was the party? _____

28 **Listen and write.**

A fun party

I ¹_____ to a birthday party at my school. The school was 50 years old. Parents and grandparents ²_____ to the school party. There ³_____ drinks and food. We ⁴_____ a lot. The teachers ⁵_____ and we ⁶_____ games outside. In the evening, we ⁷_____ and talked with friends. The bakery in our town ⁸_____ a very big cake and ⁹_____ it to the school. It ¹⁰_____ a fun party!

29 **Write about a fun party you went to.**

_____
_____
_____
_____
_____
_____
_____
_____
_____
_____
_____
_____

 Are you ready for Unit 7?

7 School

1 **Listen and write.**

The first class at school was ¹_____. The second and third classes were
²_____. There was an ³_____ game in the fourth class.
Lunch was ⁴_____, but ⁵_____, too. The classes after lunch
were ⁶_____. In the last class, we read some poems. Some were
⁷_____, some were ⁸_____, and some were ⁹_____.

2 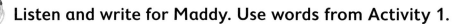 **Listen and write for Maddy. Use words from Activity 1.**

1

Maddy _____

You _____

2

Maddy _____

You _____

3

Maddy _____

You _____

4

Maddy _____

You _____

5

Maddy _____

You _____

6

Maddy _____

You _____

3 Write a word under each book in Activity 2 for yourself.

4 **Read. Then match.**

> My first day at school was scary. I was only five and there were a lot of big children in the school. The classes were very difficult. My teacher, Mr. Taylor, was friendly but I was very sad!

1 Was Emma's first day at school scary?

2 Was she four?

3 Were there a lot of big children?

4 Were the classes easy?

5 Was her teacher friendly?

6 Was she sad?

a No, she wasn't.

b Yes, he was.

c Yes, it was.

d No, they weren't.

e Yes, she was.

f Yes, there were.

5 **Unscramble and write questions about your first day at school. Then write the answers.**

1 you / how / were / old

_____

_____

2 your / patient / was / teacher

_____

_____

3 there / scary / any / were / things

_____

_____

4 you / were / happy

_____

_____

6 **Write about the first time you did your favorite sport.**

How old were you?   Who was with you?   Were you happy?

Was it exciting/scary/easy/difficult?

> The first time I played tennis, I was six years old. It was...

_____

_____

7 Find and circle six words. Then unscramble the letters that aren't circled.

IGEOGRAPHYSNMUSICSCIENCELMATHGARTEHHISTORY

What was your favorite subject last year?

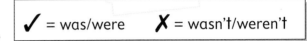

8 Write. Then listen and circle T = True or F = False.

| ✔ = was/were | ✗ = wasn't/weren't |

1 + ✔ boring _____ T / F

2 ✗ easy _____ T / F

3 + ✔ fun _____ T / F

4 ✗ interesting _____ T / F

5 + ✗ difficult _____ T / F

6 ✔ exciting _____ T / F

9 Write three sentences about your classes last week.

1 Science was _____ .

2 Math _____ .

3 _____

10   **Listen and circle. Then write.**

Dan's homework diary				
Monday	**Tuesday**	**Wednesday**	**Thursday**	**Friday**
math computer science	history geography	English science	music art	music P.E.

1 Did Dan have computer science homework on Monday? _____

2 Did Dan have geography homework on Tuesday? _____

3 Did Dan have English homework on Wednesday? _____

4 Did Dan have art homework on Thursday? _____

5 Did Dan have music homework on Friday? _____

11 Write.

Maddy's homework diary				
Monday	**Tuesday**	**Wednesday**	**Thursday**	**Friday**
music	English	computer science	math	geography art
relaxing	easy	boring	difficult	interesting

1 Maddy's homework on Tuesday was _____.

Was it difficult? _____

2 Was Maddy's homework on Thursday difficult? _____

3 Was Maddy's homework on Wednesday interesting? _____

4 Maddy's homework on Friday was _____ and _____.

Was it boring? _____

5 Was Maddy's homework on Monday exciting? _____

12 Write.

1 Did you have homework yesterday? _____

2 Was it difficult? _____

13 **Look at the story and circle.**

1   (Polly / A police officer / The Police Chief) goes into the cave first.

2   There's a (school / tunnel / party) in the caves.

3   Polly finds (the diamonds / a key / a school schedule) in the tunnel.

4   They can't go on without a (poem / code / rope).

5   Art is at (9:00 / 10:30 / 12:40).

6   It is (morning / afternoon / night) when they come out of the tunnel.

14 **Check (✓).**

1   Who is having a party?   **2**   Who is invited to the party?

15 **Write.**

> cave   great job   party   phew   tunnel

1   There is often music and dancing at a _____.

2   A _____ is a hole in a mountain that people can go into.

3   People sometimes say "_____ _____" when you do something well.

4   A _____ can go through a mountain, underground, or even under water.

5   People sometimes say " _____!" when something bad doesn't happen.

16 **Imagine. What happens next in the story?**

I think _____.

17 Unscramble and write questions about an older family member's youth.

1   was / what / favorite / your / food _____

2   color / what / favorite / your / was _____

3   favorite / who / singer / was / your _____

4   easy / you / was / for / math _____

5   star / was / your / who / movie / favorite _____

6   instrument / you / play / did / an _____

7   movies / like / scary / you / did _____

8   was / what / subject / your / favorite _____

9   you / fun / for / school / was _____

10   P.E. / at / you / good / were _____

18 Answer the questions in Activity 17 for yourself today.

1   <u>My favorite food is pizza.</u> _____

2   _____

3   _____

4   _____

5   _____

6   _____

7   _____

8   _____

9   _____

10   _____

19 Read. Then circle.

Jack: Hi, Suzy. Were you on your school trip yesterday?

Suzy: No, not yesterday. We went on Thursday. We were in New York. There were some beautiful statues and some interesting pictures, too.

Jack: Why were you there?

Suzy: It was an art trip. We're learning about artists from around the world, and New York has art from lots of different countries: Egypt, China, Spain, France, the United Kingdom, and the United States, of course.

Jack: Was it an interesting day?

Suzy: Yes, it was. It was very interesting but we were very tired after the trip. There was a lot of walking!

Jack: Walking?! I always go to New York by train.

Suzy: Yes, we went by train and then by bus. But in the afternoon there weren't any buses and it was a very long walk!

1 Suzy's school trip was (on Thursday / yesterday).

2 There were some beautiful (statues / houses).

3 It was an (art / geography) trip.

4 It was a very (interesting / boring) day.

5 The children were (excited / tired) after the trip.

6 There weren't any (buses / trains) in the afternoon.

20 Write about your school trip.

My class went on a school trip (when?) _____. It was a (what subject?) _____ trip. We went to (where?) _____. It was very (boring/interesting/relaxing/exciting/scary) _____ because _____ _____.

21 Write questions and answers about Tara.

1 any other children / on your farm ✗

<u>Were there any other children on your farm?</u> <u>No, there weren't.</u>

2 any horses / on your farm ✓

_____ _____

3 a radio / in your house ✓

_____ _____

4 any teachers / near your house ✗

_____ _____

22 Listen and write.

Star Interview!

And then we went to the United States, and I went to
¹_____ there.

²_____ **you happy at your new school?**

No, I ³_____. It was very ⁴_____ in a class
with lots of other children.

Were your teachers good?

Yes, they were. But the ⁵_____ and English classes were too ⁶_____,
and the ⁷_____ and geography classes were too ⁸_____.

What was your favorite subject?

⁹_____ – I was on the basketball team. It was very ¹⁰_____.

23 Do you want to go to Tara's school? Why? / Why not? Write.

_____

_____

24 Match.

1	funny	**a**	studying technology
2	scary	**b**	studying countries, mountains, and rivers
3	exciting	**c**	studying sounds made by instruments
4	history	**d**	Jokes should be this.
5	geography	**e**	studying things from long ago
6	computer science	**f**	a good, fun feeling
7	music	**g**	Dark places can be this.

25 Write.

Were you at home?	Yes, I was.	No, I ¹_____.
² _____ he/she happy?	Yes, he/she was.	No, he/she wasn't.
Was it interesting?	Yes, it ³_____.	No, it wasn't.
Were we tired?	Yes, we were.	No, we ⁴_____.
⁵ _____ they funny?	Yes, they were.	No, they weren't.
Was ⁶_____ a cake?	Yes, there was.	No, there wasn't.
Were there any boys?	Yes, there ⁷_____.	No, there weren't.

26 Write.

David: My school was a tennis school.

Interviewer: ¹_____ there other classes, too?

David: Yes, there were – math, science, English, and history. But they ²_____ only in the morning. There ³_____ tennis lessons every afternoon.

Interviewer: ⁴_____ it a good school?

David: Yes, it was. My sister ⁵_____ happy there, too. Her favorite subject was art but there ⁶_____ much time for art classes because we ⁷_____ practicing tennis every day. It ⁸_____ a great school for a tennis player!

27 **Listen and write.**

My favorite subjects last year

○ My favorite subjects last year were English, P.E., and ¹_____.
² _____ was good because we read a lot of ³_____ poems.
Science was ⁴_____ but the teacher ⁵_____ very good.
Her classes were ⁶_____. She's my favorite teacher.

○ ⁷_____ was fun ⁸_____ I'm good at sports. Wednesday
was my ⁹_____ day because we played sports all afternoon. P.E. was
¹⁰_____ because there were no tests.

28 **Write about your favorite subjects last year.**

_____

_____

_____

_____

_____

_____

_____

_____

_____

_____

_____

_____

_____

 Are you ready for Unit 8?

Entertainment

1 Write the nationalities in the crossword.

1 Korea

2 Egypt

3 Japan

4 the United States

5 Argentina

6 Italy

7 Colombia

8 China

9 India

10 Spain

11 Mexico

12 Brazil

13 the United Kingdom

14 Australia

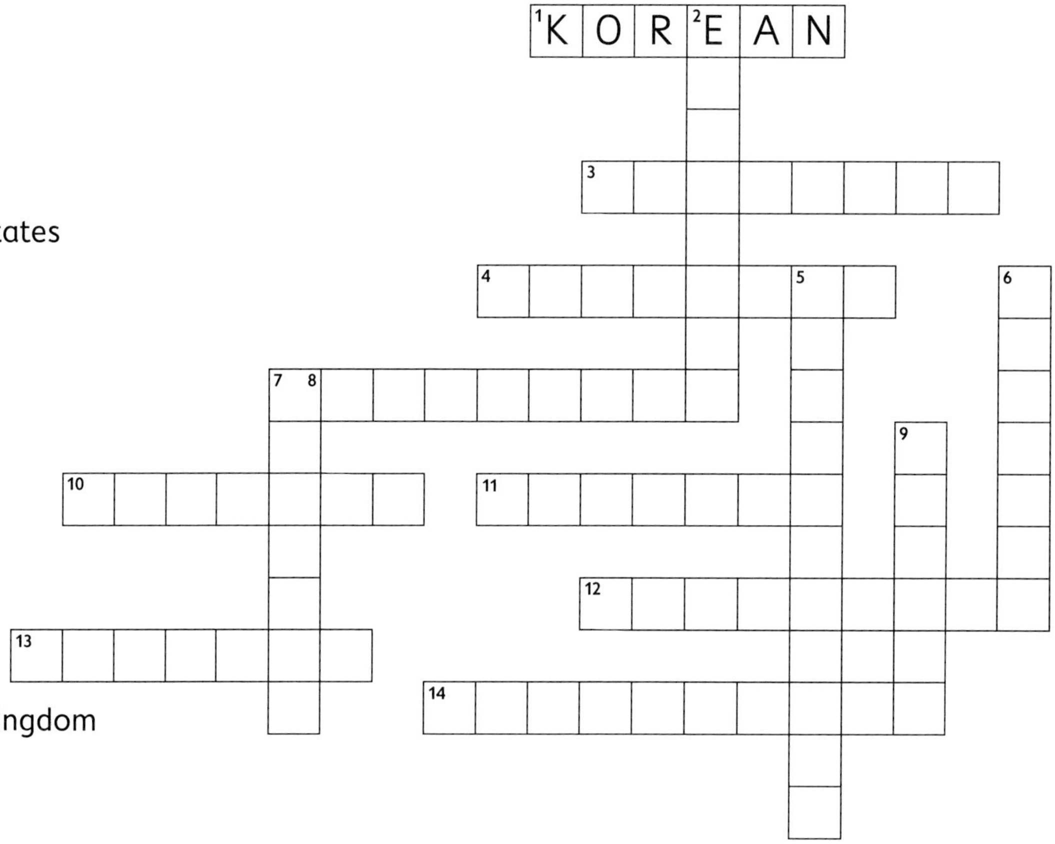

¹K O R ²E A N

2 Listen and match.

1	Nicole Kidman	Argentina	tennis player
2	J. K. Rowling	Australia	writer
3	Rafael Nadal	the United States	singer
4	Lionel Messi	Spain	soccer player
5	Beyoncé	the United Kingdom	movie star

3 Choose two people from Activity 2. Write about them.

Beyoncé is an American singer.

1 _____

2 _____

4  Listen and match.

5 Look at Activity 4 and write.

1 Where's she from? She's from _____. She's _____.

2 Is he Brazilian? _____. He's from _____.

3 Is she Egyptian? _____. She's from _____.
She's _____.

4 Where's he from? He's from _____. He's _____.

5 Is she from Argentina? _____. She's _____.

6 Where's he from? He's from _____. He's _____.

6 Find and circle. Then write.

c	o	w	b	o	y	a	c	t	o	r
d	s	a	f	a	j	g	p	t	h	u
e	o	i	k	j	r	k	c	j	i	s
y	l	t	e	s	a	i	l	o	r	p
q	d	e	l	o	a	n	c	e	r	y
u	i	r	s	f	i	g	a	c	t	o
e	e	r	m	b	q	d	n	p	c	o
e	r	s	c	i	e	n	t	i	s	t
n	c	m	u	s	i	c	i	a	n	x

(1)

_____

(2)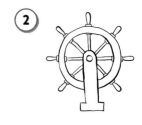

_____

(3)

_____

(4)

_____

(5)

_____

(6)

_____

(7)

_____

(8)

_____

(9)

_____

(10)

_____

7 Look and write.

> August 25th   December   night   ~~Saturday~~   seven o'clock
> the afternoon   the winter   three-thirty   Tuesday

in	on	at
_____	_Saturday_	_____
_____	_____	_____
_____	_____	_____

8 🎧 **Listen and number.**

9 **Write. Then number.**

1 Yao Ming is _____. He's from China.

He's the man _____ played basketball in the United States.

The Year of the Yao was made in 2004. It's a movie _____ tells the story of his first year in the NBA.

2 Was she _____?

Yes, she was. She was queen of Egypt.

In 51 BC she was the woman _____ ruled Egypt.

Cleopatra is a movie _____ was made in 1999. It tells Cleopatra's life story.

3 Where's he from?

He's from Brazil. He's _____.

He's the soccer player _____ Brazilians call "King Pele."

Pele Forever was made in 2004. It's a movie _____ most Brazilian boys love.

10 Look at the story and match.

1 How does the Queen feel?

a The Police Chief.

2 What does Mike do?

b The Queen.

3 How do Frost and Smith feel?

c She is amused and surprised.

4 Who says, "How extraordinary!"

d He finds the diamonds.

5 Where are the diamonds?

e They feel angry and scared.

6 Who says, "Quick! Catch them!"

f They're in the ice wall.

11 Look and write.

1

I'm _____.
I'm from _____.
Where _____?

I'm a Martian. _____
from _____.

2

_____ Canadian?
Which part of _____
are you _____?

I'm from Ice Island.
_____ are
you from?
_____ Italian?

Yes, I'm from
_____.

12 Write.

1 My favorite character is _____.

2 He/She has _____.

3 He/She is _____.

4 He/She likes _____.

13 Imagine. What happens next to the characters?

I think _____.

14 **Read and complete the chart. Who is the best role model?**

VALUES

Be a good role model for others.

Gwyneth always works hard at school and often arrives on time. Her mother works all day so Gwyneth usually helps a lot around the house. She cleans her room and makes breakfast for her younger brother.

Marcela is never on time and always late. She sometimes works hard at school but doesn't like to clean her room or help around the house, so she never does that.

Rob is always on time. He usually works hard at school and does his homework. He often helps at home. He takes out the trash and cleans his room.

Harry is usually on time but is sometimes late for class. He sometimes works hard at school and sometimes helps at home, but he really likes watching movies.

	arrives on time	works hard at school	helps at home
Gwyneth	o		
Marcela			
Rob			
Harry			

a = always
u = usually
o = often
s = sometimes
n = never

The best role model is _____.

15 **Are you a good role model? Write about yourself.**

I _____ arrive on time. _____

16 **What should you do to be better?**

I should help at home.

I should _____.

18 **Write.**

Chinese   days   exciting   famous   king   water

1   The tennis game is very _____.

2   The players in the game are Spanish and _____.

3   The movie star was a _____ in his first movie.

4   The young actor is very _____ all around the world.

5   On the island, there isn't any clean _____.

6   The girl got the fruit two _____ ago.

19 **Write about your favorite TV show.**

My favorite TV show is _____.

It's _____.

20 Circle.

¹(In / On / At) the winter, it's dark after school. I come home ²(in / on / at) 3:30 and do my homework. Then I play video games. ³(Last / Yesterday / Three) year, my favorite video game was *Nintendogs + Cats* but the game that I like now is *Scribblenauts Unmasked*. *Scribblenauts Unmasked* is a game that is popular with my friends. Two months ⁴(last / ago / then), I wasn't very good at ⁵(play / player / playing) the game. Some of the puzzles are very difficult but now I'm a good ⁶(play / player / playing). I often play ⁷(in / on / at) the evening with my friends and ⁸(in / on / at) Saturday and Sunday, too.

21 Read the puzzle. Then circle ✓ = True or ✗ = False in the quiz and write to find the answer.

This is a puzzle about a cowboy who lived in Texas.

Four days ago, the cowboy went to the city on Friday.

Yesterday, he went home on Friday. How?

Technology Quiz...

1 There were video games a hundred years ago.	✔ We	✗ The
2 There were video games in 1940.	✔ can	✗ horse's
3 Mario is a famous video game character.	✔ name	✗ act
4 Before the books and films, Harry Potter was a video game.	✔ in	✗ was
5 In FIFA video games, you play soccer.	✔ Friday	✗ films

1 ___The___ **2** _____ **3** _____ **4** _____ **5** _____

22 Match.

1   a Mexican actor
2   an Italian spy
3   an Indian soldier
4   a Japanese musician
5   an Egyptian king
6   a British queen
7   a Brazilian sailor
8   a Korean scientist

a   a person from a country in Asia who fights

b   a singer or guitar player who is from an island country in Asia

c   a rich person who is from a country in North Africa

d   a person from a country near the United States who works on a stage

e   a person from a country near Japan who is good at science

f   a rich woman who is from an island country in Europe

g   a person who lives on a ship and comes from a country in South America

h   a person from Europe who watches what some people do, then tells other people

23 Look at Activity 22 and write.

1   Is the soldier from Brazil?   _____

2   Where's the sailor from?   _____

3   Who's from Korea?   _____

4   Is the king from Italy?   _____

5   Are the spy and the queen from Europe? _____

6   Where's the musician from?   _____

24 Write the sentences using *that* or *who*.

1   the Chinese restaurant / I went to / was very good

_____

2   was good-looking / a Mexican actor / I met

_____

25  Listen and write.

My favorite entertainment

My favorite kind of entertainment is ¹_____ TV. I love watching movies at ²_____. I often watch one ³_____ many times. I like watching movies ⁴_____ are in English. My favorite ⁵_____ is Robert Pattinson because he's handsome. I ⁶_____ to music, too. I download ⁷_____ from the Internet. I love ⁸_____ music. I like playing many ⁹_____ and often play with my ¹⁰_____ in the park.

26 Write about your favorite entertainment.

Goodbye

1 Write.

1 Who are the Ice Detectives? _____

2 Where are the thieves now? _____

3 What do the children and Gizmo eat to celebrate? _____

4 Who has a new pet? _____

5 How do you know that the Queen remembers Mike and Polly? _____

6 How do the explorers know that Mike and Polly found the diamonds? _____

2 Circle.

1 Whose is this?
It's (Hector Frost's / the Queen's).

2 Where did Hector Frost first see it?
He saw it (on TV / in town).

3 Who used these?
(Smith / Hector Frost) used them.

4 What did he see through them?
He saw (a polar bear / Mike and Polly).

5 Who had this on the mountain?
(The explorers / Mike and Polly) had it on the mountain.

6 What did they use it for?
They used it for following (the road / Smith).

7 Whose are these?
They're (Mike's / Smith's).

8 Where did he use them?
He used them at (the training camp / Bollington Hall).

3 Write.

1 Were there any explorers on Ice Island? _____

2 Was there a research station on Ice Island? _____

3 Were there any pyramids on Ice Island? _____

4 Was there a volcano on Ice Island? _____

4 Circle.

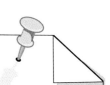

1 What's Maddy like? (Unit 1)
She's (smart but lazy / patient and funny).

2 What was Maddy doing in Unit 2?
She was (taking out the trash / doing her homework).

3 What's Robbie good at? (Unit 3)
He's good at (reading poetry / kicking balls).

4 What was Robbie doing in Unit 2?
He was (studying before a test / playing video games).

5 What does Emma look like? (Unit 1)
She has (straight / spiky) hair and glasses.

6 Emma loves shopping, but what was very expensive? (Unit 5)
The (scarf / jacket) was very expensive.

7 How much was the item that was expensive? (Unit 5)
It was (one hundred and twenty-four dollars / twelve dollars).

8 What was Emma doing in Unit 3?
She was (telling jokes / reading a book).

9 What does Kipper love doing? (Units 1, 2, and 3)
He loves (eating fish / catching birds).

10 What does Dan look like? (Unit 1)
He has spiky hair and (brown / green) eyes.

11 What was scary on the bus? (Unit 7)
A (green / blue) hand was scary on the bus.

12 What was Dan doing in Unit 8?
He was watching a (basketball / soccer) game.

13 Who's the man who must watch the soccer game because he can't walk? (Unit 8)
He's (Carlos / Mario).

14 Is Carlos from the United States? (Unit 8)
No, he isn't. He's (Mexican / Spanish).

5 **Listen and write.**

#		
1	March 1st	
2		Spain
3	March 30th	
4	April 29th	
5		Mexico
6		Argentina
7	June 21st	
8		Korea
9	July 8th	

6 **Complete your school schedule. What do you think about each subject?**

	Monday	Tuesday	Wednesday	Thursday	Friday
morning					
easy/difficult/ interesting/boring/ relaxing					
afternoon					
easy/difficult/ interesting/boring/ relaxing					

7 **Write about your daily routine.**

1 I always _____.

2 I usually _____.

3 I often _____.

4 I sometimes _____.

5 I never _____.

8 **Write.**

1 Yesterday, I _____ .

2 Yesterday, I didn't _____ .

9 **Draw or stick a picture of your favorite place. Then write.**

There's a _____ .

There isn't a _____ .

There are some _____ .

There aren't any _____ .

10 **Draw or stick a picture of your favorite famous person. Then write.**

What does he/she look like?

_____

Why do you like him/her?

_____

What is he/she good at?

_____

Where is he/she from?

_____

This is _____ .

(He's / She's) (a / an) _____ .

Structures

Welcome

- I played tennis on Monday morning.
- We cleaned our rooms on Sunday morning.
- He/She danced at the party on Friday evening.
- They went to the movies on Saturday afternoon.

Unit 1 Friends

What does he/she look like?	He's/She's good-looking. He/She has straight, dark hair and brown eyes.
What do they look like?	They're tall and good-looking. They have short, light hair and blue eyes.

He/She doesn't have light hair.
They don't have light hair.

What's he/she like?	He's sporty and he's smart.
	She's bossy but hard-working.

I like him because he's patient. I like her because she's friendly.

Unit 2 My life

- You must brush your teeth. *(Order)*
- You should brush your teeth. *(Advice)*

- I always brush my teeth.
- He usually brushes his teeth.
- She often brushes her teeth.
- They sometimes brush their teeth.
- We never brush our teeth.

Unit 3 Free time

What am I good at?	I'm good at hitting.
What's he/she good at?	He's/She's good at hitting.
What are they good at?	They're good at hitting.
He/She isn't good at catching. / They aren't good at catching.	
What does he/she like/love doing?	He/She likes/loves going shopping.

What were you doing yesterday at 7:00?	I was drawing pictures.
What was he/she doing yesterday at 7:00?	He/She was drawing pictures.
What were they doing yesterday at 7:00?	They were drawing pictures.
Were you drawing pictures?	Yes, I was. / No, I wasn't.
Was he/she drawing pictures?	Yes, he/she was. / No, he/she wasn't.
Were they drawing pictures?	Yes, they were. / No, they weren't.

Unit 4 Around the world

There's a rain forest in Brazil.
There isn't a rain forest in Korea.
There are some penguins in Argentina.
There aren't any penguins in Italy.

Is there a pyramid in the city?	Yes, there is. / No, there isn't.
Are there any beaches in Australia?	Yes, there are some beautiful beaches in Australia.
Are there any volcanoes in the United Kingdom?	No, there aren't.

Unit 5 Shopping

How much is this/that jacket?	It's ninety dollars and fifty cents.
How much are these/those sunglasses?	They're thirty dollars.

Whose watch is this?		Whose pens are these?	
It's	Maddy's. mine. yours. his. hers.	They're	Dan's. mine. yours. his. hers.

Unit 6 Party time

I made a cake.

I didn't make a cake.

Where did you go?	I went to Ghana.
When did you go to Ghana?	I went on August 1st.
What did you see?	I saw giant butterflies.
Who did you meet?	I met my relatives.

Unit 7 School

Was it interesting?	Yes, it was. / No, it wasn't.
Was there an alien in it?	Yes, there was. / No, there wasn't.
Were there any exciting stories?	Yes, there were. / No, there weren't.

Did you have computer science on Tuesday?	Yes, I did. / No, I didn't.
Was P.E. relaxing?	Yes, it was. / No, it wasn't. It was difficult.

Unit 8 Entertainment

Is he/she from the United States?	Yes, he/she is.	No, he/she isn't.
Where's he/she from?	He's/She's from Argentina.	He's/She's Argentinian.
Where are they from?	They're from Australia.	They're Australian.

He's a cowboy.	He likes playing the guitar.	He's a cowboy who likes playing the guitar.
It's an American movie.	It's very famous.	It's an American movie that's very famous.